My Homeschool

Book of Centuries

My Homeschool Book of Centuries

A timeline history tool to capture maps, moments, and memorable people through the ages.

By Michelle Morrow © 2023

1st Edition

ISBN: 978-0-9805087-6-5

All enquiries to:

My Homeschool PTY LTD,

NSW, Australia

https://myhomeschool.com

MY BOOK OF

CENTURIES

BY

"It is necessary to know something of what has gone before in order to think justly of what is occurring today."

Charlotte Mason Volume 6:169

Contents

Introduction

Charlotte Mason encouraged children to make a timeline notebook that recorded famous people, events, and dates. These books were used across all subjects and were designed to be a keepsake. The purpose of this type of book was to help children picture history chronologically. It is a child's own reference book of history which is commenced around the age of ten years old and continued throughout their education. It is usually best to allow each child to have their own book. However some families choose to make this a collective exercise and the make a Family Book of Centuries.

A KEEPSAKE

"The Book of Centuries, is a great joy to the owner, and even in these busy days it is possible to find some time, however short, to add an illustration from time to time. Children always take a keen delight in their books. There is no need to be an artist in order to have quite an interesting book—neatness and accuracy are essential though. Museums will be clothed with fresh interest to keepers of these books, who will be able to recognise objects which have already become familiar old friends through their Books of Centuries". Getrude M Bernau—Principal of the PNEU

Drawing inspiration from the time-honoured practice detailed in the Charlotte Mason Method and Classical Homeschooling, the My Homeschool Book of Centuries will transform your history studies into a creative external memory of events, people and places that can be used throughout the homeschool years.

HOW TO USE YOUR BOOK OF CENTURIES

There are five parts to this book.

- Family Timeline
- Table of Centuries
- Maps
- Book of Centuries Timeline: This part is filled out over the course of a child's education, often starting around age 10 and continuing into high school. New entries are added each year as new periods of history are studied.
- Notes: At the back of the book there is space for additional notes or sketches about history that have may not fit neatly within a particular century.

MAKING AN ENTRY

One page is a very small space in which to illustrate an entire century; thus, each child should select what they consider the most characteristic events, planning out the arrangement of the page, as much as possible, before drawing. Pencils, erasable pens, or fine ink markers are recommended. Keep entries brief. Think of this book as a personal reference with key words.

Colour illustrations can be added but make note of the paper quality being used so illustrations will not impact the other side of the page.

FINDING ANCIENT HISTORY DATES & ARCHAEOLOGY

Archaeology is a science dating from the 1800's. It is historic in nature and often the findings are more assumptions based on theory rather than repeatable testing to examine a hypothesis. For this reason, archaeologist's findings are often arbitrary and can vary. Take the city of Nineveh as an example; for many years archaeologists claimed that it did not exist then it was discovered by Austen Henry Layard in 1847. Therefore, we recommend using a consistent source for dates. Possible options are:

The time scale in the My Homeschool Book of Centuries includes the following periods:	
BC	Before Christ
B.C.E	Before Common Era or Before Christian Era. These are the same as BC.
AD	Anno Domini (Latin for after Christ or In the Year of Our Lord).
C.E	Common Era is the same as AD it is just the non-religious version
Pre History	Before 3000BC (Early Civilisations in Mesopotamia)
Ancient History	3000BC to 600BC (The Greek Era)
Classical Era	600BC to 476AD (Fall of Rome)
Middle Ages	476AD to 1450AD (The Printing Press)
Early Modern Age	1450AD to 1750AD (Industrial Revolution)
Modern History	1750 to Present time
Note: Parenthesised events are the trigger to define the next era.	

- The Annuals of World by James Ussher (Begins 4000BC using the Bible as a reference)
- Cassell's Chronology of World History by Hywel Williams (Secular history begins at 8000 BC)
- https://humanhistorytimeline.com/

Family History Timeline

100 YEARS OF FAMILY HISTORY

The family history chart is a place to record significant events the family consider important. Whilst it can be a family project, it is not a family tree.

Here are some ideas of what you might like to include in your family history:

⇒ Family birthdates and death dates, such as those of siblings, parents, and grandparents. Make the entry short, recording the name of the person. For example, [name's] birthday.

⇒ Family holidays: mention the location. For example, ['Gold Coast holiday'].

⇒ Important family events such as getting a dog, moving house, or weddings.

⇒ Significant health events such as having an operation, breaking a limb, or getting glasses.

⇒ Local weather/nature events that impacted your location. For example, flood in town, bushfire nearby, or mouse plague.

This is a linear chart that allows for more freedom marking in events that happen close together. Make an entry on the page and then draw a line to the relevant point on the timeline.

This project will be a work in progress and can be continued throughout the years.

EXAMPLE

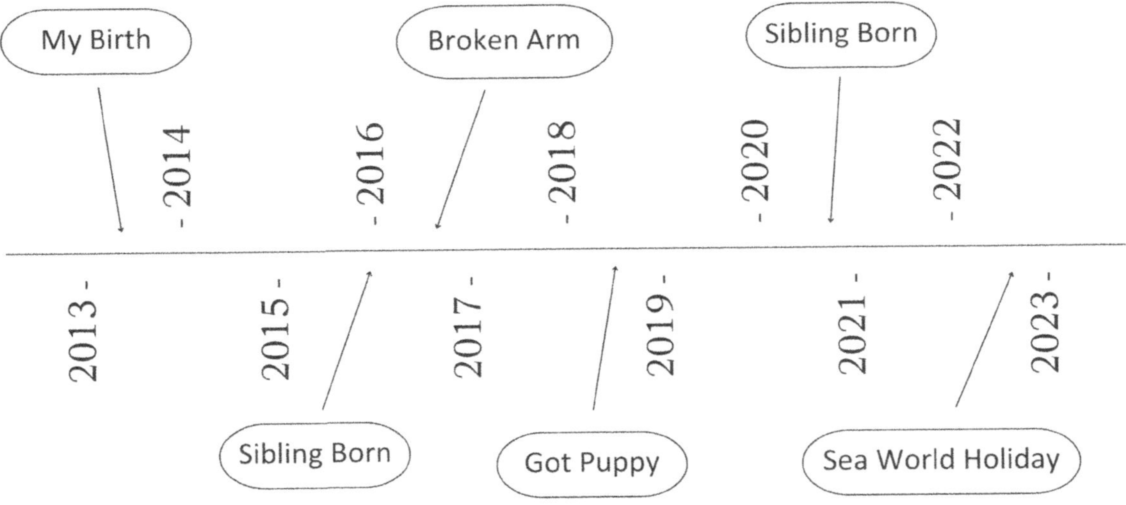

Family History Timeline

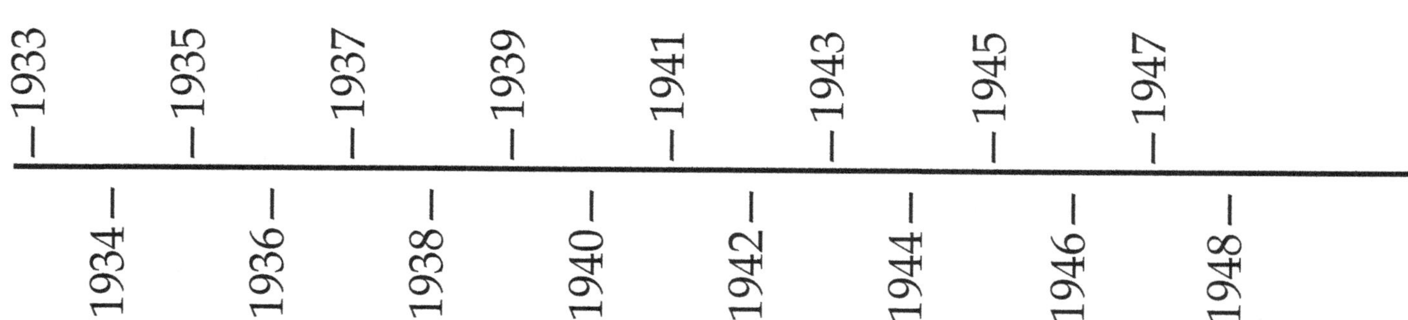

100 Years of Family History

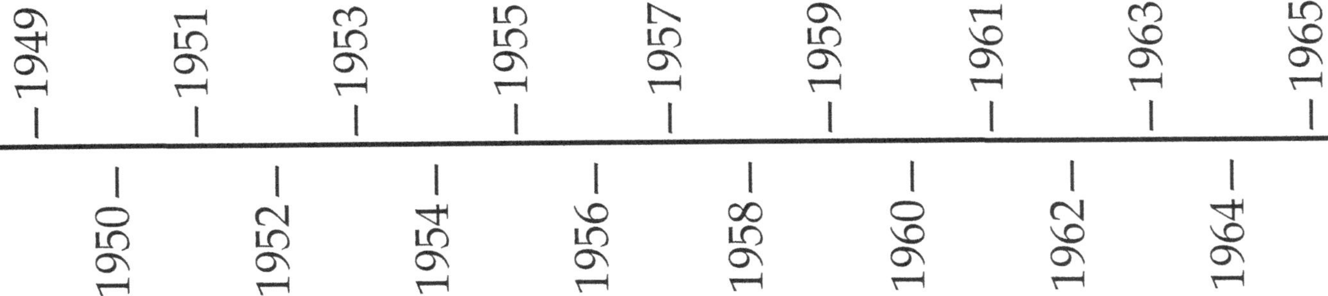

Family History Timeline

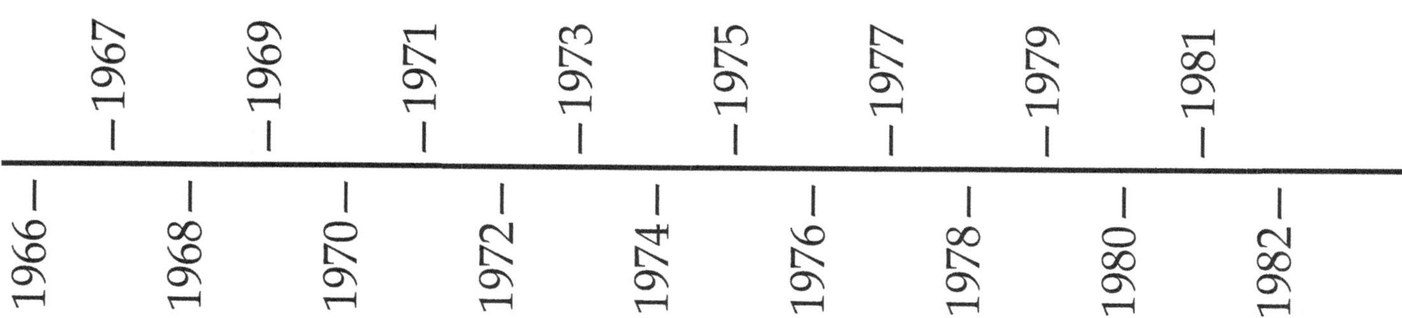

100 Years of Family History

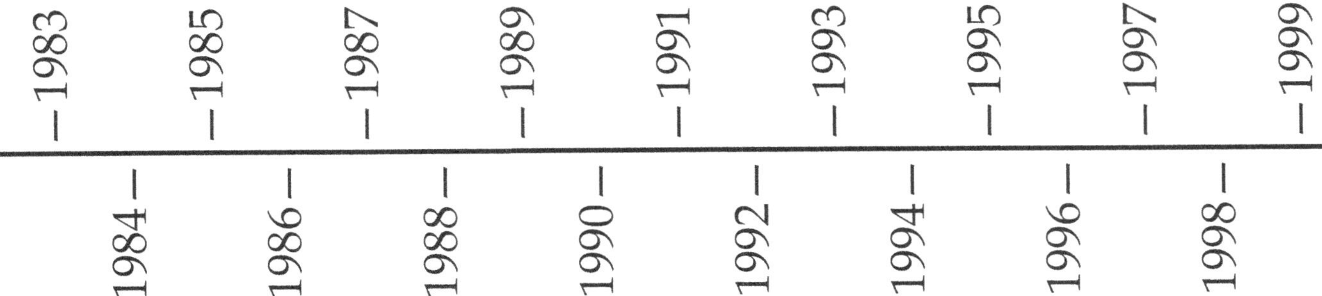

Family History Timeline

2000
2001
2002
2003
2004
2005
2006
2007
2008
2009
2010
2011
2012
2013
2014
2015
2016

100 Years of Family History

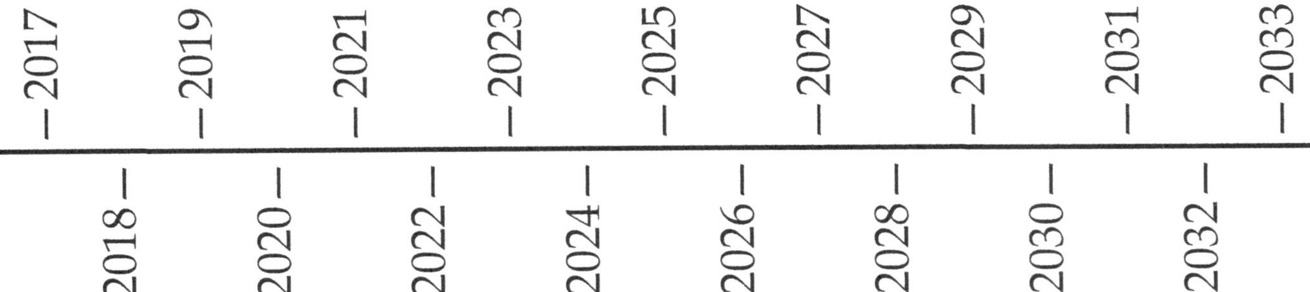

Table of Centuries & Maps

Here you record significant people in a century. This table acts as a quick reference. Only a name is required, and no dates are needed.

CALCULATING CENTURIES

It can be confusing when referring to specific centuries as there are two ways to calculate centuries. The method we have used here is to calculate a century from '01' to '100' in the year the new century begins. For example, the 1st Century begins with AD 1 and ends in 100AD. The 20th Century began in 1901AD and ended in 2000AD. We are currently living in the 21st Century.

SUGGESTED ABREVIATIONS

b.	Born (date someone is born)
d.	Died (date someone died)
r.	Reigned (Use for kings, queens, presidents, prime ministers and other rulers)
c.	About that time. Circa is a word of Latin origin meaning 'approximately'.

EXAMPLE:

If you use an abbreviation you will solve the dilemma of people living in two centuries, for example the birth of Queen Elizabeth II (1926 AD) and her death was in (Death 2022).

3rd Century BC	Alexander the Great	d. Plato
1st Century AD	d. Jesus	Nero
20th Century AD	b. Elizabeth II	
21st Century AD	d. Elizabeth II	r. Donald Trump

MAPS

Four blackline World Maps have been provided. Use these to record name changes of places over the centuries.

Suggested map ideas for this section:

⇒ Ancient History Map—The Ptolemaic map is a 2nd century map showing the world as flat. It indicates the places that were known to exist at that time.

⇒ Medieval Maps—For example the world during the Roman Empire. You could also include religious and mythological elements. The Mappa Mundi is a great one to explore.

⇒ Navigation Charts —Follow the routes of different explorers and expeditions such as Lewis and Clarke, Captain Cook, Christopher Columbus or Bass and Flinders.

⇒ Migration, Colonisation and Imperial Maps—Track the expansion of people groups such as the Table of Nations depicted in the Bible after the flood of Noah, Viking expeditions, Polynesian expansion across the Pacific, and pre and post Colonisation maps.

Additional pages are provided to draw maps of cities, coastlines, or travel routes. You may also like to draw a map within a specific century. For example: tracking a battle during a wars, a specific exploration like Lewis and Clarke in Africa, Bass and Flinders around Australia, or the partition of India in 1947.

Table of History BC

4000 – 3501						
3500 – 3001						
3000 – 2501						
2500 – 2001						
20th | 2000 – 1901						
19th | 1900 – 1801						
18th | 1800 – 1701						
17th | 1700 – 1601						
16th | 1600 – 1501						
15th | 1500 – 1401						
14th | 1400 – 1301						
13th | 1300 – 1201						
12th | 1200 – 1101						
11th | 1100 – 1001						
10th | 1000 – 901						
9th | 900 – 801						
8th | 800 – 701						
7th | 700 – 601						
6th | 600 – 501						
5th | 500 – 401						
4th | 400 – 301						
3rd | 300 – 201						
2nd | 200 – 101						
1st | 100 – 1						

Table of Centuries AD

1st | 01-100						
2nd | 101–200						
3rd | 201–300						
4th | 301–400						
5th | 401–500						
6th | 501–600						
7th | 601–700						
8th | 701–800						
9th | 801–900						
10th | 901–1000						
11th | 1001–1100						
12th | 1101–1200						
13th | 1201–1300						
14th | 1301–1400						
15th | 1401–1500						
16th | 1501–1600						
17th | 1601–1700						
18th | 1701–1800						
19th | 1801–1900						
20th | 1901–2000						
21st | 2001–2100						

MAPS THROUGH THE AGES

World Map Date:______________________

MAPS THROUGH THE AGES

World Map Date:________________________

MAPS THROUGH THE AGES

World Map Date:___________________

MAPS THROUGH THE AGES

World Map Date:____________________

Book of Centuries

TIME PERIOD DIVISIONS

There are two page spreads for each time period.

- Pre History is not dated and you will find there are various archaeological interpretations.
- 4000BC – 2000BC are set out in 500 year periods because there isn't a lot of recorded history for this period.
- From 1999BC – 1899AD history is set out in a century (100 years) format.

PRE HISTORY

The Pre History period does not specify dates and you have more flexibility in presentation. Some people like to theme these pages with titles such as The Ice Age, Bronze Age, Ancient Egypt, or Creation stories. It's up to you.

ADDING DATES

You'll find dates in many books that you read, not just history books. Start filling in your dates as they are discovered in history, science, art, the Bible, a museum visits, or wherever you come across them in other parts of your learning journey.

EXAMPLE ENTRY 5TH CENTURY AD

Make entries in the appropriate row. Use abbreviations previously mentioned in the *Table of Centuries* (page 17). Sometimes, you may have more than one entry in a row, so be succinct. When you don't have an exact date (like there isn't for Saint Patrick) use approximate dates. You can mentally divide each row period into five sections. For example in 430AD you can see there are two entries. Vandals lay siege on Rome n 430 AD and Attila becomes leader of the Huns in 433AD.

410	Visigoths sack Rome
415	
420	c. St Patrick Ireland
425	
430	Vandals siege Rome | r. Attila the Hun

430	431	432	433	434

ADDING ILLUSTRATIONS

In each century, a space is provided to add illustrations to the period you are learning about. Adding illustrations to a Book of Centuries is meant to be a thoughtful pleasurable event. You do not need to be an artist to make an intriguing book, but neatness and precision is important.

Your Book of Centuries can be filled out in two ways. The first is to list important dates, and the second is to add illustrations of these occurrences. For example, when learning about the Australian bushrangers you may like to draw Ned Kelly's famous helmet. Symbols, quotations, short lists or maps are also good for reluctant drawers.

Originally called a Museum Notebook, the Book of Centuries was a place to sketch out items discovered whilst visiting a museum. Getrude Bernau, the principal of girls school in London would often take her students to the British Museum and get them to make entries in their Museum Notebooks. She wrote an article for the Charlotte Mason publication *A Parent's Review* (Volume 34: 1923) about creating a Book of Centuries. Here is a summary of her ideas with some additional practical tips:

⇒ When adding illustrations use mainly black and white with occasional colour. Note: Using a monochrome colour scheme makes the book look homogonous. **Pencil sketches are best** . Ink drawings (which were suggested by Gertrude) are better on thicker art paper and pasted into your book.
⇒ Illustrations found in books and symbols are often a good source of inspiration. [Online image searches can also be helpful].
⇒ When the subject is too difficult to sketch, photographs can be pasted in, but only seldom, as it makes the book excessively thick.
⇒ Since reading should be a lifelong interest, kids should wait until they can handle harder topics.
⇒ One page is a little space to represent a century so the most important events should be sketched and the page's design layout should be planned if possible.
⇒ Some children like to illustrate one topic throughout the book, such as clothing, flags, ships, weaponry, musical instruments, or ornaments of different centuries, in addition to the customary illustrations of each century's events. No two books will be alike!
⇒ An example page from the 9th century AD might include: a Danish battle-axe, byrnie, ship, helmet, ring-money, Saxon harp and ship, and King Alfred's jewel and silver penny.

To see examples and illustrations check out:
https://myhomeschool.com/homeschooling/programs/book-of-centuries

Pre History

We call events prehistory when they occurred before stories were written down. It's when things happened, but there are no written words to tell us about them. Instead of using written records historians use different clues like objects and bones. However, these are not always as reliable as written records. The first records of writing that have been discovered are from the Egyptians around 3200BC and that is where the prehistory period ends.

Pre History

Pre History

Pre History

Pre History

Pre History

40th – 36th Century BC

4000 - 3501 BC

4000

3950

3900

3850

3800

3750

3700

3650

3600

3550

35th – 31st Century BC

3500– 3001 BC

3500

3450

3400

3350

3300

3250

3200

3150

3100

3050

Ancient History

Ancient history from 3000BC to 600BC spans a critical period marked by the rise and fall of civilisations across the globe. During this time, various cultures made significant advancements in politics, technology, and culture, leaving a lasting impact on the course of human history.

MESOPOTAMIA

In the Fertile Crescent region, also known as Mesopotamia, (modern-day Turkey, Iraq, Kuwait, and Syria), several major civilisations emerged. The Sumerians developed one of the world's earliest systems of writing, known as cuneiform, and established city-states like Ur and Uruk. The Akkadian Empire, under the rule of Sargon the Great, unified Mesopotamia into one of the first known empires. The Babylonians, led by Hammurabi created the famous Code of Hammurabi, one of the earliest known legal codes. These developments laid the groundwork for organised societies and legal systems that would influence later civilisations.

EGYPT

In ancient Egypt, the Old Kingdom witnessed the construction of monumental pyramids, such as the Great Pyramid of Giza, a testament to the Egyptians' advanced engineering and organisational skills. Egypt's rulers, known as pharaohs, held divine authority, and their elaborate burial practices reflected their belief in an afterlife. Hieroglyphic writing and complex religious practices characterised this era, contributing to Egypt's unique cultural identity.

HEBREWS

In the ancient Near East, the Hebrews, led by figures like Abraham and Moses, embarked on a journey that would eventually lead to the formation of monotheistic Judaism. The Hebrew Bible, with its foundational texts like the Torah, contains the religious and historical narratives of the Hebrew people. Their belief that there is only one God and ethical teachings would have a profound influence on later Abrahamic religions, including Christianity and Islam.

ASSYRIANS AND BABYLONIANS

The Assyrians, centred in the region of modern-day Iraq, established a formidable empire known for its military prowess and ruthless conquests during the 2nd millennium BC. They were succeeded by the Babylonians, who captured Jerusalem in 587BC and forced the exile of the Hebrews, an event remembered as the Babylonian Captivity. The Babylonians are also famous for their advanced knowledge of astronomy and mathematics.

CHINA

In ancient China, the Shang Dynasty introduced early forms of Chinese writing and bronze casting. This period laid the foundation for the complex societal structures and philosophies that would come to define Chinese civilisation. The Zhou Dynasty succeeded the Shang and introduced the concept of the "Mandate of Heaven," which justified the ruling dynasty's authority based on the will of divine forces.

THE CELTS

The Celts were a diverse group of ancient peoples who inhabited parts of Europe. They were known for their distinctive culture, art, and language, which was the precursor to modern Celtic languages like Irish, Welsh, and Scottish Gaelic. The Celts were not a unified empire or nation but rather a collection of tribes and communities spread across regions that include modern-day Ireland, the United Kingdom, France, Spain, and parts of Central Europe.

ABORIGINAL AUSTRALIANS

In the vast continent of Australia, Aboriginal peoples developed rich and diverse cultures over thousands of years. These Indigenous societies, with their unique languages, spiritual beliefs, and intricate art forms, adapted to the diverse landscapes of Australia. They practiced sustainable hunting and gathering, demonstrating a deep understanding of their environment.

NORTH AND SOUTH AMERICA

In North America, civilisations like the Mississippian culture and the Ancestral Puebloans developed complex societies with distinctive art and architecture, while the Iroquois Confederacy introduced early forms of representative governance. Along the Pacific Northwest coast, indigenous tribes had intricate trade networks and cultures centred around fishing. In South America, the Inca Empire thrived with advanced administrative systems and monumental architecture, while the Moche culture left behind impressive pottery and pyramid constructions. The ancient Americas were characterised by rich cultural diversity and remarkable achievements, which laid the foundation for the complex histories of these continents.

THE GROWTH OF CIVILISATIONS

In summary, the period from 3000BC to 600BC was a time of remarkable cultural, political, and intellectual development in various parts of the world. From the emergence of early civilisations in Mesopotamia and Egypt to the formation of monotheistic beliefs among the Hebrews, and the rise of powerful empires like the Assyrians and Babylonians, this era set the stage for the complex and interconnected history of human civilisation. Meanwhile, in China, Europe, Australia and North and South America distinct cultures and traditions were flourishing, contributing to the rich tapestry of human history. These ancient societies left an enduring legacy that continues to shape our understanding of the past and our world today.

30th – 26th Century BC

3000 - 2501 BC

3000

2950

2900

2850

2800

2750

2700

2650

2600

2550

25th – 21st Century BC

2500 - 2001 BC

2500

2450

2400

2350

2300

2250

2200

2150

2100

2050

20th Century BC

2000 - 1901 BC

95

85

75

65

55

45

35

25

15

5

19th Century BC

1900 - 1801 BC

95

85

75

65

55

45

35

25

15

5

18th Century BC

1800 - 1701 BC

95

85

75

65

55

45

35

25

15

5

17th Century BC

1700 - 1601 BC

95

85

75

65

55

45

35

25

15

5

16th Century BC

1600 - 1501 BC

95

85

75

65

55

45

35

25

15

5

15th Century BC

1500 - 1401 BC

95

85

75

65

55

45

35

25

15

5

14th Century BC

1400 - 1301 BC

95

85

75

65

55

45

35

25

15

5

13th Century BC

1300 - 1201 BC

95

85

75

65

55

45

35

25

15

5

12th Century BC

1200 - 1101 BC

95

85

75

65

55

45

35

25

15

5

11th Century BC

1100 - 1001 BC

95

85

75

65

55

45

35

25

15

5

10th Century BC

1000 - 901 BC

95

85

75

65

55

45

35

25

15

5

9th Century BC

900 - 801 BC

95

85

75

65

55

45

35

25

15

5

8th Century BC

800 - 701 BC

95

85

75

65

55

45

35

25

15

5

7th Century BC

700 - 601 BC

95

85

75

65

55

45

35

25

15

5

6th Century BC

600 - 501 BC

95

85

75

65

55

45

35

25

15

5

The Classical Era

The Classical Era, often dated from approximately 500BC to 476AD represents a pivotal period in human history characterised by remarkable advancements in culture, politics, philosophy, and technology. This era, which spans several centuries, saw the rise and fall of influential civilisations, the emergence of profound philosophical thought, and the development of enduring artistic and architectural masterpieces.

THE GRECO-ROMAN LEGACY

The Classical Era is often associated with the civilisations of ancient Greece and Rome, which made profound contributions to the world. In Greece, the 5th century BC marked the "Golden Age," with Athenian democracy flourishing under the leadership of figures like Pericles. The period gave birth to Greek philosophy, with luminaries like Socrates, Plato, and Aristotle laying the foundations for Western thought. These are the men Plutarch, the Ancient Greek historian, wrote about in his collection of biographies called *Parallel Lives.*

Additionally, the Greek city-states engaged in cultural achievements, producing timeless works of literature, such as the epics of Homer, and groundbreaking art and architecture exemplified by the Parthenon.

Rome, on the other hand, began as a republic and transitioned into an empire. The Roman Republic introduced the concept of checks and balances in government and the rule of law, ideals that continue to influence modern governance. Under the Pax Romana, a period of relative peace and stability, the Romans constructed an intricate road system, aqueducts, and monumental architecture like the Colosseum and the Pantheon. The Roman legal system, known as Roman Law, still forms the basis of many legal codes today. The decline of the Roman Empire in the 5th century AD marked the end of this classical period in Europe.

THE BIRTH AND DEATH OF JESUS

The birth and death of Jesus Christ holds profound historical significance within the Classical era. These events, occurring amidst the turbulent backdrop of the Roman Empire, marked the emergence of Christianity as a transformative religious and cultural force. Jesus' teachings, emphasising love, forgiveness, and spiritual redemption, resonated with diverse audiences across the Roman world, challenging the prevailing religious and social norms. His crucifixion under Pontius Pilate and the subsequent spread of Christianity throughout the Mediterranean and beyond altered the course of history, eventually leading to the adoption of Christianity as the state religion of the Roman Empire in the 4th century CE, profoundly influencing the subsequent development of Western civilisation and shaping the world for centuries to come.

The transition from BC (Before Christ) to AD (Anno Domini, which means "In the Year of Our Lord" in Latin) marks a pivotal point in history. It signifies the shift from dating events based on years before the estimated birth of Jesus Christ to dating events from his birth onward.

THE MAURYAN AND GUPTA EMPIRES IN INDIA

In India, the Classical Era witnessed the rise of two major empires: the Mauryan Empire and the Gupta Empire. The Mauryan Empire, under the rule of Emperor Ashoka, expanded across the Indian subcontinent and promoted Buddhism as a major religion. Ashoka's edicts, inscribed on pillars and rocks, are significant historical documents that promoted moral governance and tolerance.

The Gupta Empire, which emerged in the 4th century AD, is often referred to as India's "Golden Age." During this time, India made significant advancements in mathematics, particularly the concept of zero and the decimal system. Literature, including the famous works of Kalidasa, and art, notably the construction of the Ajanta and Ellora Caves, flourished. The Gupta era is remembered as a period of intellectual and cultural achievement.

ANCIENT CHINA AND THE QIN DYNASTY

Classical China, during the Zhou and Qin dynasties, contributed substantially to the era's intellectual and technological advancements. The Chinese philosopher Confucius promoted moral ethics and social harmony through his teachings. Legalism, another school of thought, emerged during this time, emphasising strict laws and centralised authority.

The Qin Dynasty, is particularly significant for unifying China under a single centralised government. This period witnessed the construction of the Great Wall of China, an iconic architectural marvel still standing today. It also marked the standardisation of weights, measures, and writing scripts.

THE CLASSICAL ERA BEYOND THE MEDITERRANEAN AND ASIA

While Greece, Rome, India, and China are often the focal points of the Classical Era, other civilisations and regions also played critical roles. In the Americas, the Maya civilisation in Mesoamerica and the Nazca culture in South America developed advanced societies with complex calendars, mathematics, and monumental architecture.

THE CLASSICAL ERA'S LEGACY

The Classical Era stands as a testament to human ingenuity and cultural achievement. It was a period of enlightenment, innovation, and the creation of enduring legacies in politics, philosophy, science, art, and architecture. The contributions of Greece, Rome, India, and China, among others, continue to influence and shape our modern world, making the Classical Era a pivotal chapter in the narrative of human history.

5th Century BC

500 - 401 BC

95

85

75

65

55

45

35

25

15

5

4th Century BC

400 - 301 BC

95

85

75

65

55

45

35

25

15

5

3rd Century BC

300 - 201 BC

95

85

75

65

55

45

35

25

15

5

2nd Century BC

200 - 101 BC

95

85

75

65

55

45

35

25

15

5

1st Century BC

100 - 1 BC

95

85

75

65

55

45

35

25

15

5

1st Century AD

01 - 100 AD

5

15

25

35

45

55

65

75

85

95

2nd Century AD

101 - 200 AD

5

15

25

35

45

55

65

75

85

95

3rd Century AD

201 - 300 AD

5

15

25

35

45

55

65

75

85

95

4th Century AD

301 - 400 AD

5

15

25

35

45

55

65

75

85

95

The Middle Ages

The Middle Ages, often referred to as the Medieval Period, spanned roughly from the 5th to the 15th century in Europe. This thousand year period of history is a time of turbulence, triumphs and transformations. This period begins in the aftermath of the Roman Empire's collapse, around the 5th century, where Europe's destiny hung in the balance.

As you fill your *My Homeschool Book of Centuries* you will encounter key dates and players. Here is a brief summary of this period.

THE DAWN OF THE DARK AGES

As the Roman Empire crumbled, Europe plunged into chaos. The once-mighty Roman legions retreated, leaving a power vacuum. Barbarian tribes like the Visigoths, Vandals, and Ostrogoths carved out their kingdoms from the ruins. It was a time of tumultuous migrations and shifting borders.

THE RISE OF CHARLEMAGNE AND THE HOLY CATHOLIC CHURCH

In the heart of this turmoil emerged a remarkable figure, Charlemagne. Charlemagne, crowned as the Holy Roman Emperor in the 8th century, sought to restore order and unity to Western Europe. He ushered in the Carolingian Renaissance, a brief revival of art, culture, and learning.

The Roman Catholic Church became a towering institution, offering spiritual solace and guidance. Monasteries became beacons of knowledge and culture, where monks meticulously copied and preserved ancient manuscripts.

FEUDALISM AND THE MANOR

The feudal system, a defining feature of the Middle Ages, structured society into a hierarchy. At the apex stood the king, followed by nobles, knights, and peasants. In exchange for protection, peasants worked the land and paid tribute to their lords. The manorial system, which operated alongside feudalism, revolved around self-sustaining agricultural communities.

THE CHURCH'S INFLUENCE

The Pope wielded significant political and spiritual power, shaping the destiny of kings and kingdoms. The Catholic Church codified canon law, its own legal system, and fostered intellectual inquiry through scholasticism. The Church also initiated the Crusades, a series of holy wars aimed at recapturing Jerusalem from Muslim control.

Medieval Europe left a lasting legacy in the realm of art and architecture. The soaring cathedrals, characterised by Gothic architecture's pointed arches and ribbed vaults, reflected the people's profound religious devotion. Illuminated manuscripts, epic poems, and intricate paintings adorned this era.

RENAISSANCE AND TRANSITION

Despite the challenges of the Middle Ages, there were sparks of innovation. Scholars like Avicenna and Roger Bacon made strides in medicine and natural philosophy. Universities emerged, paving the way for the Renaissance, a cultural and intellectual reawakening.

As the Middle Ages drew to a close, Europe faced formidable trials. The Black Death, a devastating plague, and ravaged populations brought misery. The Hundred Years' War between England and France, spanning the 14th and 15th centuries, reshaped the political landscape.

THE ROAD TO MODERNITY

The late Middle Ages saw the beginnings of a transformation. Feudalism waned as centralised monarchies and urban centres gained prominence. The Renaissance blossomed, marking a resurgence in art, science, and literature. It was a harbinger of the modern world.

ASIAN EMPIRES AND RELIGION

Asia during the Middle Ages was a diverse and vibrant continent marked by the rise of influential empires and the exchange of culture and knowledge along the Silk Road. China's Tang Dynasty flourished, fostering art and innovation, while the Byzantine Empire acted as a bridge between Europe and Asia. South Asia saw the Chola Dynasty's maritime influence and the spread of Buddhism to Southeast Asia. Central Asia played a crucial role as a trade crossroads, and the Islamic Caliphates in Baghdad advanced various fields of knowledge.

Japan during the Middle Ages, which corresponds to the period between the 12th and 16th centuries, is often referred to as the "Feudal Era" in Japanese history. This era was marked by the dominance of the samurai warrior class, the rise of powerful feudal lords, and significant cultural developments.

THE SOUTH PACIFIC

South Pacific exploration was marked by the navigational prowess of Polynesian seafarers who undertook incredible journeys across vast ocean expanses. These intrepid explorers, using advanced navigational techniques, explored and settled islands across the South Pacific, such as Hawaii, New Zealand, and Easter Island.

THE LEGACY OF THE MIDDLE AGES

The Middle Ages, despite its darkness and challenges, left an indelible mark on Western civilisation. It was a period of growth, decline, and rebirth. From the ashes of the Roman Empire, Europe forged new identities and laid the foundations for the modern era. The Middle Ages, with all its complexity and contradictions, remains a captivating chapter in the grand story of human history.

5th Century AD

401 - 500 AD

5

15

25

35

45

55

65

75

85

95

6th Century AD

501 - 600 AD

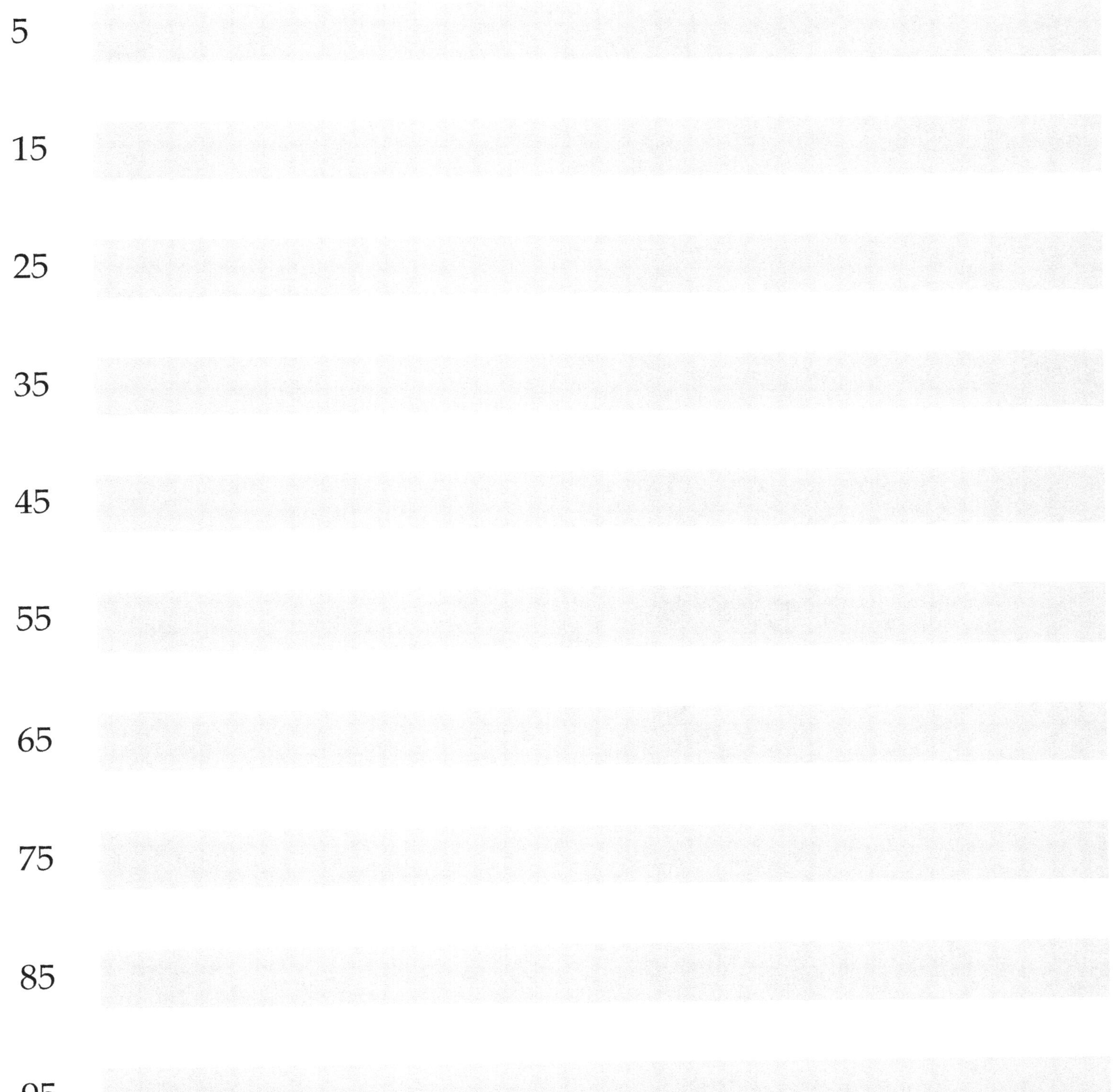

7th Century AD

601 - 700 AD

5

15

25

35

45

55

65

75

85

95

8th Century AD

701 - 800 AD

5

15

25

35

45

55

65

75

85

95

9th Century AD

801 - 900 AD

5

15

25

35

45

55

65

75

85

95

10th Century AD

901 - 1000 AD

5

15

25

35

45

55

65

75

85

95

11th Century AD

1001 - 1100 AD

5

15

25

35

45

55

65

75

85

95

12th Century AD

1101 - 1200 AD

5

15

25

35

45

55

65

75

85

95

13th Century AD

1201 - 1300 AD

5

15

25

35

45

55

65

75

85

95

14th Century AD

1301 - 1400 AD

5

15

25

35

45

55

65

75

85

95

Early Modern Age

The Early Modern Age, spanning from approximately 1450AD to 1750AD, was an exciting chapter in human history. It's characterised by profound changes in politics, society, culture, and economics. It marked the transition from the medieval world to the modern era, with several key developments shaping this transitional period.

The Age of Exploration

European powers, driven by a thirst for wealth, knowledge, and the desire to find new trade routes, embarked on extensive voyages. Notable explorers like Christopher Columbus, Vasco da Gama, and Ferdinand Magellan navigated uncharted waters, leading to the discovery of the New World (the Americas) and the establishment of global trade networks.

The Renaissance

The Early Modern Age saw the flowering of the Renaissance, a cultural and intellectual movement that revitalized art, science, and learning. Renaissance artists like Leonardo da Vinci and Michelangelo created masterpieces. Humanism, a focus on human potential and achievement, became a central theme.

The Reformation

The religious landscape was dramatically altered by the Protestant Reformation initiated by Martin Luther in 1517. This movement led to the schism within Christianity, with the emergence of various Protestant denominations challenging the authority of the Roman Catholic Church. The Reformation had profound political and social implications, sparking religious wars and reshaping the European map.

Colonialism and Empires

European powers, particularly Spain, Portugal, England, France, and the Netherlands, established vast colonial empires during this period. Colonisation had far-reaching consequences, including the exchange of goods, cultures, and diseases between the Old World and the New World, the exploitation of indigenous peoples, and the accumulation of immense wealth by European colonial powers.

Missionary Movements

European powers, particularly Spain and Portugal, dispatched missionaries across the globe as they expanded their empires, leading to the Christianisation of indigenous peoples in the Americas,

Africa, and Asia. The Jesuits, a prominent Catholic order, established a global presence with their highly educated and disciplined missionaries, while Protestant denominations also engaged in evangelical efforts. These missionaries often accompanied explorers, establishing religious cultural footholds in newly discovered lands. This contributed to the spread of Christianity and played pivotal roles in education and healthcare.

Scientific Revolution

The Early Modern Age witnessed the Scientific Revolution, marked by advancements in mathematics, astronomy, and physics. Figures like Galileo Galilei, Isaac Newton and Copernicus formulated groundbreaking theories that laid the foundation for modern science.

The Enlightenment

Towards the end of this era, the Enlightenment emerged as a philosophical and intellectual movement that emphasized reason, liberty, and individual rights. Thinkers like Voltaire, John Locke, and Jean-Jacques Rousseau questioned existing institutions and advocated for political and social reforms.

Absolutism and Constitutionalism

Various forms of government emerged during this period. Absolute monarchies, exemplified by Louis XIV of France, centralized power in the hands of rulers. However, in some countries like England, the Glorious Revolution of 1688 led to the establishment of constitutional monarchies, where the power of monarchs was limited by representative institutions.

Shaping The Modern Era

In summary, the Early Modern Age was marked by profound changes in exploration, culture, religion, science, and governance. It set the stage for the modern world by reshaping Europe's relationship with the rest of the world, challenging traditional norms and beliefs, and paving the way for the development of modern nation-states and the scientific method. This transitional period laid the groundwork for the subsequent developments that would shape the modern era.

15th Century AD

1401 - 1500 AD

5

15

25

35

45

55

65

75

85

95

16th Century AD

1501 - 1600 AD

5

15

25

35

45

55

65

75

85

95

17th Century AD

1601 - 1700 AD

5

15

25

35

45

55

65

75

85

95

18th Century AD

1701 - 1800 AD

5

15

25

35

45

55

65

75

85

95

Modern History

Modern history refers to the period from approximately the mid-18th century to the present day. It is characterised by significant social, political, economic, and technological changes that have shaped the contemporary world. This era includes pivotal events such as the Industrial Revolution, the spread of democracy, the rise and fall of empires, and the advent of globalisation and digital technology. Modern history encompasses the evolution of political ideologies, the struggles for civil rights and gender equality, and the ongoing challenges and opportunities that define our current global society.

THE AGE OF REVOLUTION

The late 18th century saw the American Revolution and the French Revolution, which inspired ideals of liberty, equality, and fraternity. These events led to the spread of republicanism and the decline of absolute monarchies, setting the stage for modern democracies.

THE INDUSTRIAL REVOLUTION

The Industrial Revolution transformed economies and societies through the mechanisation of agriculture and industry, leading to urbanisation and the growth of the working class. Innovations like the steam engine, textile machinery, and the telegraph revolutionised production and communication.

COLONIALISM AND IMPERIALISM

European colonial powers expanded their empires across Asia, Africa, and the Pacific, leading to the exploitation of resources and the suppression of indigenous cultures. British colonization of North America laid the foundation for the American War of Independence. The conflict was fuelled by American grievances over British taxation, perceived tyranny, and a desire for self-governance, ultimately leading to the birth of the United States of America in 1776. British expansion then moved to setting up colonies in Australia and New Zealand .

The scramble for Africa and the Opium Wars in China also happened during this era of imperial domination.

COMMUNISM

The rise of communism emerged in response to industrialisation and capitalism. It gained momentum through the 1917 Russian Revolution, leading to the Soviet Union, the first communist state. Communism spread to countries like China under leaders like Mao Zedong. Despite its promise of equality, communism often led to authoritarianism, human rights issues, and ideological conflicts, leaving a lasting mark on modern history.

WORLD WARS AND THE AFTERMATH

The 20th century was marked by two devastating world wars. World War I and World War II resulted in immense human suffering including the Holocaust. This led to the reshaping global politics and the founding of the United Nations to promote international cooperation and prevent future conflicts.

The aftermath of World War II witnessed the dismantling of colonial empires. India gained independence from British rule in 1947, and other nations followed suit in Asia, Africa, and the Middle East, ushering in an era of decolonisation.

THE COLD WAR AMD THE SPACE RACE

The Cold War emerged as a global ideological and political struggle between the United States and the Soviet Union, characterised by the space race, the arms race, proxy conflicts, and the division of the world into two opposing blocs. The fall of the Berlin Wall in 1989 and the dissolution of the Soviet Union in 1991 marked the end of this era.

CIVIL RIGHTS MOVEMENTS

The struggle for civil rights gained momentum in the 20th century, with movements like the American Civil Rights Movement and the anti-apartheid movement in South Africa challenging racial discrimination and segregation.

GLOBALISATION AND TECHNOLOGY

The 20th and 21st centuries witnessed remarkable technological progress. The invention of the internet and the proliferation of computers and smartphones transformed communication, commerce, and social interaction, leading to the digital age and globalisation. This intensified economic interdependence, cultural exchange, and the flow of information worldwide. It brought both opportunities and challenges, contributing to economic growth while exacerbating income inequality and cultural homogenisation.

ENVIRONMENTAL CONCERNS

The latter half of the 20th century and the 21st century have seen growing awareness of environmental issues. Concerns about climate change, pollution, and resource depletion have led to efforts to address sustainability and environmental conservation.

HISTORY EVOLVES

In summary, modern history from 1750 to the present day is marked by an array of transformative events, from revolutions and industrialisation to world wars and globalisation. It reflects the evolving nature of human society and the complex challenges and opportunities that have shaped our contemporary world. The legacies of this period continue to influence political, social, and technological developments as we navigate the complexities of the 21st century.

19th Century AD

1801 - 1900 AD

5

15

25

35

45

55

65

75

85

95

20th Century AD

1901 - 2000 AD

5

15

25

35

45

55

65

75

85

95

21st Century AD

2001 - 2100 AD

5

15

25

35

45

55

65

75

85

95

Made in the USA
Las Vegas, NV
03 September 2024

94756185R00079